KELI MARIE

Safeguarding Your Child's Spiritual Health

A guide in your journey to better protecting your child's spiritual health

CURATED SHOPPE
PRESS

I dedicate this book to:

God, as a fulfillment to my "assignment."

My children El and Addi, I pray that the foundation we are laying will always guide them in their spiritual journey.

To my husband, Roberto, I am forever grateful to do this life and parenting thing with you. I don't know anyone with greater faith than you, and I count myself blessed to have you.
Obrigado e eu te amo, querido.

Contents

Foreword

In the beginning, when I first felt God had laid it on my heart to write this book, I wondered what made me qualified to write such a book. I am no pastor, and I don 't consider myself to be any kind of a saint, matter a fact, I think of myself as pretty rough around my Christian edges. I am definitely a sinner, still searching for my perfection, as my husband likes to say. Despite feeling inadequate, and after procrastinating on my assignment from God, He made it very clear to me that He had given me this assignment, and I needed to be obedient in delivering. He even brought me to a sermon by a well-known pastor that talked about God using many people in the Bible who also felt inadequate for the job He had given them. So, here we are. I am humbly submitting to the world my " assignment," with the hopes that it will be accepted with an open heart and an open mind. So who am I to be giving anyone advice on spiritual health? Well, first off, lets first clear up the fact that I would like you not to think of this book as me giving you advice. I would instead want you to consider this my personal plea to try and persuade more parents to give greater attention to the spiritual health of our children. I firmly believe that if we as parents gave as much attention to our children's spiritual health as we do their physical health, the world would be in a much better place. Sometimes it feels like we as Christians tend to get busy in our day to day lives and forget about the spiritual war going on around us every day. A lot of times, our children, much like ourselves, can tend to get caught in the crossfire and become innocent victims of the spiritual battles happening each day. We, as parents, have been charged by God to raise and take part in not only their physical protection but also their spiritual protection. By the looks of our youth today, it seems a great deal of us are failing in protecting our "babies " on the spiritual front. It may be because we are uneducated in how to protect them, the importance of protecting them, or maybe we have just become too distracted to make their spiritual protection a priority. So, I humbly submit this plea to you, in hopes that it serves as a place of inspiration or as a guide in your journey to becoming better at safeguarding your child(ren)' s health. I hope that more parents will begin to give their children's spiritual health just as much, if not more priority, as they do their physical health. I believe if people put as much effort into learning how to spiritually protect their children as they do in learning how to protect them physically, the world will be in a much better place.

I

Spiritual Health

1

Why is the Spirit Significant: Eternal Life vs. Earthly Life

"Then shall the dust return to the earth as it was: and the spirit shall return unto God who gave it."-Ecclesiastes 12:7 (KJV)

The reason your spirit is important is pretty self-explanatory from this verse alone. The dust of your flesh will return to the ground, but your SPIRIT will return to live an everlasting life once it returns to our Maker. Your spirit is eternal. Think about that. Let it sink in, the word ETERNAL. That means imagine the rest of your life and how long you feel like that might be, and then your death, and beyond that is the rest of eternity. Something you can not see, but you know it has no end. THAT is how long your spirit will exist beyond the death of your body. THAT is why your spirit is so significant. We need to ensure that we take care of our spirit in this physical life so that it can persevere long into the afterlife. For our Spirits to persevere as needed, it helps to have a strong spiritual foundation.

Having a strong foundation as a child will help as one spiritually matures to endure the turbulent atmosphere that comes along with spiritual growth.

"If thy children will keep my covenant and my testimony that I shall teach them, their children shall also sit upon thy throne forevermore."- Psalms 132:12 (KJV)

We, as parents, have been given the assignment when God blessed us to become parents, to give our children the proper foundation. If we are obedient to this assignment, we can impact their spiritual well being, not only in this life but eternally. This could very well be the most critical job God will ever give us as people, yet so many of us give the responsibility no sense of urgency.

We are living in a day where we have no more significant time than now, to put some urgency in understanding the importance of this assignment. Kids today are becoming further and further spiritually lost, with less of a spiritual foundation than ever, it seems. I do not know how many times I have seen something in the news, which had me at a point where I felt like the person committing some horrific crime was soulless and completely taken over demonically. Our babies are falling to the wayside of a spiritual war because we, as parents, are becoming spiritually lazy in our assignment to prepare them with a strong spiritual foundation. We need to act with urgency parents.

Please take a moment and pray with me:
"God help each and every one of us parents, do justice by you in parenting these children that ultimately belong to you, but you have so graciously blessed us to have the honor of raising under your guidance. Help us to be ever watchful and spiritually open to the things that you have set before us, to be able to teach them in accordance with your Will. We pray this prayer in your Son, Jesus Christ's name. Amen."

As parents, we want to ensure our children are healthy as soon as we know they are growing in the womb. We make doctor appointments, take prenatal vitamins, and do everything in our power to ensure our growing babies and children are as healthy as possible. I remember when I became pregnant for the first time with my son, I did countless research throughout my pregnancy on how to maintain my growing baby's health best. I even pestered my husband about what I thought he should research and read to help nurture me during the pregnancy to ensure the baby's health.

However, my husband and I weren't only concerned about our son's physical health, and we were also just as adamant about our son's spiritual well being while I was pregnant. We had both been educated somewhat on spiritual warfare and wanted to ensure nothing negative or demonic taking hold around/within us, would pass to him. Since our child would be living in my womb for many months, we prayed daily for God to protect him from anything that was not of Him, living within me spiritually. There are many parents, however, that forget about their child's spiritual health. It is understandable because we don't usually have people reminding or asking us about our child's spiritual health. Also, some parents are simply unaware of the need to protect their children spiritually.

The spiritual health of children is so overlooked in so many families, and honestly, it is pretty saddening. It is saddening to me because I would challenge that your child's spiritual health is just as, if not more important than your child's physical health. Our spirits live on for eternal life, whereas our bodies are a temporary place for our spirits to reside while we are here on Earth. If this is the case, then why would we not be more concerned about our eternal spirit, then we would be our temporary bodies?

Don't misinterpret me, I am not saying that our physical health isn't important, because it is, as it is a gift from God. We should honor the gift by treating it kindly and appreciating the blessing that is life here on Earth. However, I believe that we get too caught up in our Earthly Life that we forget that there is a spiritual world coexisting simultaneously every day. We do not have to dwell in the spiritual realm, but we must not forget, because when we forget, we make ourselves vulnerable in the spiritual war. I want my children to be safe in this world and the spiritual world. There are so many dangers that lurk in not only the dangers of the street but also the dangers of spiritual darkness. The bible says:

" We wrestle not against flesh and blood, but against principalities, against powers, against the rulers of the darkness of this world, against spiritual wickedness in high places."-Ephesians 6:12 (KJV)

It is our job as their parents to protect them from ALL dangers, not just the ones of the physical world. It is also our responsibility to teach our children how to protect themselves spiritually. Our son struggles with thoughts of death and what life will be like once he is dead. These thoughts started occurring when he was about seven years old, and would only happen sparsely in the beginning, but then they became more frequent. He would usually start crying hysterically, to the point that it would take us a bit of time to calm him back down.

My husband and I knew that his mind was under spiritual attack, so we would pray for him on our own, and try and comfort him as best we could. However, we wanted him to be able to provide himself comfort, as well as help him feel powerful enough within himself to take control of his thoughts so that he wouldn't reach the point of hysteria. So I taught him something that I had learned back in college, which always helps me even still today whenever I feel fearful or as though I am under spiritual attack in my mind. I told him to sing songs of praise to God whenever he begins to have those thoughts or feels afraid. He and our daughter both know a handful of songs by heart, as I used to sing them to them as babies as a way of a lullaby. I sing these songs, to try and ward off anything that was not of God, that may be lurking in the "spiritual darkness." This technique has always worked for me, and I believe it is because of the way that it was explained to me when we sing songs of praise unto the Lord, the devil flees. He can not stand to hear us giving God praise. (You can find the list of songs we use, at the end of the book.)

Sometimes I would feel as though when I began to sing the songs of praise, that the fearful thoughts would become louder, so I would, in turn, sing louder to God, and every time it worked! Now that I have equipped my son with this tool, we challenge him to use it anytime he says he is having those thoughts. While writing this book, I decided to ask my son his own opinion on the technique and its effectiveness for him personally. He answered that he feels like when he sings the songs, they make him feel calm, and when he prays, he feels protected. He didn't have to wait for me to pray for him to cover himself in protection. He was able to call on the Holy Spirit' s protection all on his own. This is precisely the kind of spiritual empowerment we need to reinforce in our children while they are young.

* * *

<u>Things to Consider/Actions to Take:</u>

Something to consider as you continue through this book is how much significance you are giving your own spiritual growth. Looking at your current life, do you feel like you make your family's spiritual health a priority? If not, what has been holding you back or distracting you? If yes, what has been a motivator for you, and how can you try and influence a friend or family member who you think may not understand the importance?

I would challenge you to pray and meditate on three goals for yourself in spiritual growth. Maybe it is as simple as setting a reminder on your phone to read your bible every day, or committing to a time of prayer. It also could be a more significant commitment of signing up for a deliverance class. What three goals can you commit to?

How do you feel that you have been spiritually impacting your child? Do you feel like you had a good spiritual foundation from your own parents?

Depending on your answers to the previous questions, how do you plan to improve upon that foundation or lack of foundation with your own child?

2

What is a "healthy spirit"?

The Many Parts Of Us

"But I say, walk by the Spirit, and you will not gratify the desires of the flesh. For the desires of the flesh are against the Spirit, and the desires of the Spirit are against the flesh, for these are opposed to each other, to keep you from doing the things you want to do."- Galatians 5:16-17 (NIV)

A healthy spirit is a spirit at peace. It is nourished, full of goodness, love, and purpose from God. A healthy spirit emulates love, confidence, and empathy towards others. Have you ever met a person with a spirit that glows? Much like healthy skin can appear to glow, a healthy spirit can also glow. Part of living with a healthy spirit is living in tune with the Holy Spirit. The Bible tells us on several occasions that the Holy Spirit dwells within us. In 1 Corinthians 6:19, it says, "What? know ye not that your body is the temple of the Holy Ghost which is in you, which ye have of God, and ye are not your own?" I like to believe that the Holy Spirit is our connection to life all around us. In John 14:26, Jesus says, "But the Comforter, which is the Holy Ghost, whom the Father will send in my name, he shall teach you all things, and bring all things to your remembrance, whatsoever I have said unto you." I believe when we are in tune with the Holy Spirit, it helps us to discern things within our own spirit, which can help guide us throughout our lives. It can help us to discern right from wrong, when someone needs compassion or love, and helps us to understand our purpose in this life. Over the years, I have come to believe that three parts make us who we are as a whole being. There is the Holy Spirit dwelling within us, our own spirit, and lastly, the flesh. Here is my take on how all three work together:

- The Holy Spirit is our connection to God and helps us to discern things, both in the spiritual and physical world. (I also like to think of the bond/alignment between the Holy Spirit and our own spirit as our spiritual immune system.)
- Our spirit is really who WE are. It is the part of us that represents our personality, character, and decisions. It is what makes us different from one another and where our free will is exercised. Our spirit determines how we process the world around us again, both in the spiritual and physical world. I personally have found it much harder to discern things in the spiritual world, when I am not in tune with the Holy Spirit.
- Then there is our flesh. Our flesh is our whole being's way to become tangibly connected to the physical world around us. Our decisions can be influenced by how we tangibly engage with the world through our flesh.

A good analogy I think, to illustrate my thoughts on this, would be to think of a captain in her boat at sea. If the sea represents the world, then the ship would be our flesh in contact with the sea. The captain represents our spirit navigating the ship, and the captain's compass would be the Holy Spirit, giving guidance. The captain ultimately is the one who chooses how to navigate the ship in the sea. However, she can choose to trust the direction of the compass or follow the current the ship is influenced by when making her decisions.

As our children grow, even while still in the womb, many things will influence them in both the spiritual and physical world. It is our duty as parents to continually cover them in prayer, and to be their "spiritual doctor," if you will, to ensure they have the necessary "preventive care" to keep their spirits healthy.

"Dear friend, I hope all is well with you and that you are as healthy in body as you are strong in spirit."-3 John 1:2 (NIV)

* * *

Spirit of Peace

"Now the Lord of peace himself give you peace always by all means. The Lord be with you all." -2 Thessalonians 3:16 (KJV)

One of the signs of a healthy spirit is a spirit at peace. I once heard that the word Shalom, which means peace in Hebrew, was used not only as a greeting during biblical times, but was also intended as a blessing. To be at peace meant to be whole and to be living in God's will. According to the Bible, in many different verses, it mentions that God is the source of our peace. It is essential to pray for peace regularly. I would like to think that children are born spiritually at peace. When we are that small, our needs are so simple. All we need it seems is love, food, comforting, and diaper changes on occasion. However, as we grow in mind, that peace in our spirit that we are born with becomes more and more challenged, and our spiritual health can become compromised. From my understanding, the opposite of being at peace is being anxious. There are many things that we can take in both spiritually and physically that can cause us to become spiritually "infected" and can make our spirits anxious or at unrest. As adults, when our spiritual peace becomes challenged or compromised, we pray and seek God for guidance and healing. However, for our children, if we haven't taught them yet how to pray and seek God, then they do not know who to go to for the necessary remedy. So then they act out, due to that spiritual anxiety/or infection that they may be experiencing. That is why we as parents, must cover our children in prayer regularly, just like we regularly give them vitamins to strengthen their immune systems.

Can you imagine where you would be as a person if you didn't have spiritual peace within you? Have you already been living with spiritual anxiousness, or lived with it in the past? I have lived with it and sometimes fall back into it, and it can be unnerving and frustrating. If you too know what this feels like, then I am sure you can imagine what your child might be feeling when they don't have peace within their own spirit. Sometimes, when my husband and I watch our children acting out, with no rational explanation, we go to God and pray for peace in their spirit. (Although, sometimes I have to go to God in prayer first for myself because I need Jesus to be a fence all around my nerves!) It is important to note that my husband and I also check our children on their behavior in conjunction with prayer. They need to understand that they have to learn to control their behavior as best as possible, despite whatever may be going on spiritually. I like the idea that we are addressing their behavior mishaps, both on the spiritual and the physical front.

So, you may be wondering by now, "….but what does that peace look/feel like?" In all honesty, I think ultimately, it looks different for each individual, but I think the feeling is pretty much the same for all. When I am spiritually at peace, I feel content and free of anxiety. I feel fulfilled within my spirit. As in, I am not seeking anything because I recognize I have all I need. I feel gratitude in abundance. Gratitude to the point that I am in no shortage of things to thank God for, and I feel humbled by His love and care for me. That is what the feeling of contentment looks like for me. What it looks like for you may be different, and you may get to the place of peace differently from the next person. However, ultimately, we all feel contentment and fulfilled when we have spiritual peace.

I reach this place of contentment best when I set aside time for me and God to have alone time. In that alone time, I usually will start with some scripture to reflect over. Sometimes I flip through a couple of scriptures until something speaks to my spirit. (and sometimes nothing does, and do it again the next day) Usually, once something does speak to my spirit, I start to let God work through my thoughts and emotions with me, helping me to confront the things that I may not be wanting to deal with. Usually, I come back to a place where He reminds me that no matter what He loves me and that His love is sufficient to cover me through whatever journey or restlessness I am allowing to conflict with me.

Honestly, the reminder of this also helps me to, in turn, remind my own kids of the same thing. When they are feeling stressed about something or upset with themselves for messing up, I tell them that no matter what, God will still always love them and provides them Grace to mess up. I remind them that they don't have to beat themselves up for making mistakes, just like God tells me in our alone time. This reminder gives them the same kind of peace that I receive when God reminds me. Ultimately, throughout both my spiritual journey and my parenting journey, God has been teaching me how to be a better parent spiritually by setting an excellent example within He and I's relationship.

$$* * *$$

Things to Consider/Actions to Take:

I hope that you now have a better understanding of what a healthy spirit should feel like. Thinking about what a healthy spirit feels like, how would you rate your spiritual health? (Circle One)

1-Lost/Restless, 2-Restless, 3-Numb, 4-Happy but not Content, 5-Content

Why did you choose this rating?

Where do you think your child's spiritual health is? (Circle One)
1-Lost/Restless, 2-Restless, 3-Numb, 4-Happy but not Content, 5-Content

Why did you choose this rating?

Using my analogy earlier, of the captain in her ship at sea, rather than the sea being the world, what if the sea was your family's home. Is there anything in your home that you think maybe negatively influencing you or your child's spiritual health? If so, is it something you can change?

 Whether you feel like it is something you can change or not, I would challenge you to take that thing keeping your family from peace, to God in prayer and ask Him to help you to remove it from your life if it is in His will.

I pray right now, as I write this, that Lord you strengthen the reader in being confident in your ability for them and their family to be free from the bondage of whatever is holding them back from the peace that you are willing to provide if they would let it go and hand it over to you. Thank you, God, for the peace that you are helping them to gain by embarking on this journey with you, to become a better spiritual warrior for the child or children that you have entrusted to them, and for themselves. I also pray that you would encourage them in spirit to believe that they are not only capable but equipped to be the best parent that you have called them to be, and help them to know that they are enough when they live in your Grace and learn to love themselves and those around them as you have called us to love. Thank you, Father, in our Savior Jesus name, Amen.

II

The War on "Spiritual Germs"

3

Spiritual Infections- The truth and how to handle

Don't Be Spooked Out- Germs Are Icky But They Have To Be Handled

"When the unclean spirit is gone out of a man, he walketh through dry places, seeking rest; and finding none, he saith, I will return unto my house whence I came out. And when he cometh, he findeth it swept and garnished. Then goeth he, and taketh to him seven other spirits more wicked than himself; and they enter in and dwell there: and the last state of that man is worse than the first."-Luke 11:24-26 (KJV)

Demonic Spirits are real. Say it, believe it, and then let go of whatever fear you may have about it. In Part One, we discussed what a healthy spirit looks like and how it is influenced. I eluded to the idea that our spirits can become spiritually infected or compromised, which can sometimes happen because of other spirits.

Usually, when people begin to discuss demons and evil spirits, people react in a couple of ways. One they become afraid and start to fall into a mini internal panic. Another response is that some people choose to regress into a denial state, as though denying demonic existence will just make them go away. I remember when I was in college, I was a part of this on-campus bible study group. I was relatively new in my faith and had not ever met anyone who spoke about demonic spirits and spiritual warfare. So I was both spiritually and mentally unprepared when one bible study meeting became heavily focused on demonic strongholds and possessions. I was even more surprised when we were called to the prayer circle and asked to join in prayer against these demonic spirits. What I felt was full-blown fear and skepticism. One, what did these people mean when they said demonic spirits are taking a home in people? Are their demons in my classroom? Is anyone going to walk around and randomly flip out with black eyes and soul snatching? Also, do I need to stay away from dark places and shadows? Will demons start lunging out at me when I walk home at night? All these things and many more had me living in a cloud of fear.

However, God has not called us to live in a spirit of fear. So we do not need to be afraid of demonic spirits and the spiritual war going on around us, Jesus has already died and blessed us with the victory.

"Behold, I give unto you power to tread on serpents and scorpions, and over all the power of the enemy: and nothing shall by any means hurt you." -Luke 10:19 (KJV)

Now that you have hopefully smoothed past any initial fear let's get down to what you should know. Demonic spirits are much like germs and infections to me. They like to attach to a host and then try to make a home. You can have symptoms of demonic influence, and in some cases, you can even feel physically sick from demonic presence. If you are like me, the first image that comes to mind after reading that previous sentence are images of the Exorcist! Yet, let's remember that it is a movie meant to scare people. For me, and from what I have seen and experienced, handling demonic presence, once discovered, is much like treating a cold or any other illness of the body.

For instance, when your child complains of a tummy ache, you probably have a routine that you follow. It may be something like checking for a fever, having them lie down and rest, giving them vitamin C, or ibuprofen if there is a fever. Then you continue treatment until you see improvements, and then you follow up with vitamins to help boost your child's immune system. Pretty simple and not too scary.

The same method can be applied to a child dealing with demonic influence in the form of jealousy. Once you notice the symptoms, the first thing to do is to begin to pray over the child, asking God to help cleanse/deliver their spirit, and to cover them in the blood of the lamb. You will also want to expose them to the word of God, explicitly dealing with the spirit of jealousy. My personal favorite is to sing songs giving God praise because it will ward off the enemy as we talked about in an earlier chapter.

I will give an example of when we had to deal with this in our own home. When our children were recently going through a period of blatant disobedience, and showing no remorse, we went through this practice with them. It was mostly with our son; however, we noticed after a couple of weeks, our daughter began to behave in the same way, testing our authority in our home. So we begin to pray and ask God to help us to have the patience not just to reprimand them verbally and take away privileges, but also to try and remain calm enough to deal with this on a spiritual front as well. We also made sure that during our nightly prayer time, the kids also prayed something from their heart in regards to helping them be more obedient. In addition to praying, we printed out a list of bible verses dealing with obedience. Every night when they did their 20mins of reading for homework, we allowed them to use some of the time to read the verses. They had to pick one to memorize each week until we got through them all. Then we would share our verses with one another each day to see how we were progressing on memorizing our verse of the week. (Notice I said, "we." We also took part in the activities.) In the car on the way to school, instead of playing our usual secular playlist, we switched to our Christian playlist and favorite sermons. After a week, we begin to see improvements in their obedience.

Now there are several reasons why this works. Not only are we dealing with their symptoms on a spiritual level by praying and warding off spirits that are not of God, but we are also helping them to change in their own hearts. Exposing them to God's word, and allowing them to have His word stay on their mind, helps them on a subconscious level. When you ingrain God's word into your mind and your heart, I believe it helps you to be better in tune with the Holy Spirit living within us. This, in turn, helps us to make better decisions in what we allow to influence and guide us. God's word works as a vitamin in this scenario. My husband and I are boosting our children's spiritual immune system (or helping them to be better in alignment with the Holy Spirit living within them) by pumping them full of great pieces of the Word. Overall this will help them ward off anything that may try to come in contact with their spiritual system that doesn't belong there.

However, just like if we stop getting regular vitamins, our immune system will become depleted and weakened in its defense system, the same is true of the spiritual immune system. If we stop giving our children "spiritual vitamins," then we weaken the spiritual bond between their spirit and the Holy Spirit. If that bond is weakened, then they can't tap into discernment of the Holy Spirit against spiritual attacks. Looking at it again from the perspective of us being captains (our spirit) in our ships (our body), there are all kinds of other sailors out in the sea of the world that will try and influence how your child steers their ship. Also, other spirits would like to come on board your child's ship like a pirate, and take over and influence your child to trust them and their compass, instead of your child's compass.

Nonetheless, in regards to demonic spirits, although they may sound scary and you may think you have no power, recognize that they operate much like an infection or germ trying to make a home in your body. It is your job to protect yourself and your child's spiritual immune system. It can be an exhausting job sometimes, depending on what kind of "spiritual illness" you might be dealing with. Yet, the same holds true for physical illnesses, and we don't just give up and ignore those. We deal with them, because we love our kids, and that is what parents do.

✳ ✳ ✳

Things to Consider/Actions to Take:

What types of demonic or negative influences have you noticed in your own children or yourself, that you may not have taken into consideration before?

Do you feel more confident in dealing with demonic or negative spiritual influences, after reading this chapter? (Circle One) YES NO

Why did you choose the answer you chose?

**NOTE: No matter which answers you chose, if you would like to learn more about demonic warfare, a great book that I used to become more educated is called:
"Pigs in the Parlor: A Practical Guide to Deliverance" by Frank and Ida Hammond**

What types of routines would you like to add to your family's rituals, to boost your children's spiritual immune systems? List at least 3:
(i.e., reading scripture as a family, listening to your favorite Christian Playlist on your morning commute, playing bible trivia (fave at our house))

4

Transference of Spiritual "Germs"

"But every man is tempted, when he is drawn away of his own lust, and enticed.
Then when lust hath conceived, it bringeth forth sin: and sin, when it is finished,
bringeth forth death."-James 1:14-15 (KJV)

No one likes being sick. As parents, when our children are sick, we can sometimes feel powerless in being able to help them. Demonic and negative spirits transfer from person to person daily through exposure with other people who have not spiritually guarded themselves. We have to do our do-diligence as parents to ensure we cover our children in prayer to keep them protected from the "spiritual germs" that might try and infect them.

When people speak about Spiritual Transference, sometimes people imagine transference in the way of physical contact. However, after spending time in prayer and the Bible on this matter, I think the transference happens more in alignment with the above verse from James chapter 1. I believe gates are open through sin, and if someone that you associate with happens to be struggling with demonic influence or providing residency for a specific type of spirit, then a transference can occur through the gate you opened through your own sin. As Christians, we are saved, and the devil and his followers have no rights to us, under biblical law. However, when we sin, we expose doorways that invite those un-godly spirits into us. Those spirits once they attach to us, try to make a home, much like a virus does. Once the unwanted spirit becomes comfortable in us, we begin to see the symptoms that something is wrong, through behaviors, and speech. This is the case for both you and your child. Yet, just like viruses can be more detrimental in a child's system, the same is true for ungodly spirits. Just as a child's immune system gets more durable as they grow, so does a person's spiritual immunity.

Children are very impressionable, and they are continually trying to figure out the world around them. So, it is easier for them, when not appropriately guided, to become swayed or exposed by un-godly spirits. Most children struggle with disciplining themselves and practicing self-control. These are two very vital characteristics in trying to protect oneself from spiritual transference. This is where you help guide your child in understanding how to fight against and protect themselves from transference.

As the bible says:

"Train up a child in the way he should go: and when he is old, he will not depart from it." -Proverbs 22:6 (KJV)

* * *

The Plague of our Youth Today

Unfortunately, many of our children today are already spiritually sick. There is a plague of entitlement, lack of compassion, rebellion, self-worship, and many other illnesses of the spirit. The problem is too many parents either don't understand their children are spiritually sick, or they are too busy to dig deeper and connect with God for understanding for themselves, let alone for their children. (Being busy is something I let distract me regularly.)

It doesn't help that spiritual health isn't made as much of a priority as physical health in everyday society. When we go to take our kids for checkups, our doctors remind us, or strongly suggest to us vaccinations and medications to keep our kids physically healthy. Besides, when we think about spiritual health, it is more times than not, something we think about in regards to self-healing and self-improvement. Rarely is it thought about in regards to ensuring that we are trying to teach our children, or something that we should be working to help our children learn preventive care measures.

Sometimes we as the parents are the ones who transfer "spiritual germs" or infections to our children. If we are carrying around our own spiritual illness, that we haven't addressed, it becomes very easy to transfer to our children. This is usually more likely to happen I believe if we aren't making our kid's spiritual health a priority. Children learn from us, and if we are teaching them behaviors that will allow them to open the same gate for demonic or negative influence, then it will happen more than likely. Some parents' spiritual illnesses can stem from childhood transference from their own family members. There can be spiritual illnesses that were passed along from their grandparents to their parents. If no one in the family ever recognizes that the transference is happening to every generation, nor tries to change it, then it can continue happening for generations. These types of spiritual transferences can sometimes be called "generational curses." "Generational Curses" can plague a family for years. Spirits of incest, addiction, depression, are just a few of these kinds of curses.

* * *

Protecting the Circle

An essential part of protecting your child from spiritual transference is protecting your child's circle. Within my circle of friends and family, I have always been known as a protective mom. My protectiveness is sometimes misinterpreted as me wanting to protect my children from everything "bad" in the world. Yet, this isn't the case. I am perfectly aware that I can not, nor would I want to protect my children from everything "bad" in this world. I actually believe that we do our children a disservice when we try to protect them from everything. Children need to endure and go through adversity, in some ways, because as many Christians know, it is through our trials and tribulations that we achieve spiritual growth. Sometimes we can very well be trying to protect our child from something that God is trying to teach them something through. Remember, God is ultimately your child's true parent. We, as parents, have merely been gifted/chosen to assist God in the raising of His children.

Nonetheless, in regards to my husband and I assisting God in raising our children, we take protecting our children's circle very seriously. The reason is that as I said earlier, children are still very impressionable in their adolescent and pre-teen years. Even though my husband and I are giving them their spiritual "vitamins" at home and doing our best to teach our kids how to choose their friends wisely, they still have to contend with peer pressure, social media, and stereotypes. All of which sometimes have their own underlying spiritual influences that aren't always in alignment with God. So, in our home, there are some general rules in regards to socializing with friends and using social apps.

One of the most significant rules that we get the most flack about from both our kids and other parents is that in general, our kids aren't allowed to spend the night at other people's homes. This will be the case until we feel secure that our kids can spiritually discern on their own, an environment, or a person. Right now, our kids are still learning how to hear the voice of God within their personal relationship with Him. We have always expressed to them how it is so important for them to build a relationship with God of their own—making sure to distinguish the difference between building a relationship with God, versus having a routine of attending church and memorizing the Word. Building a relationship with God will strengthen them in understanding the lessons and wisdom in God's Word, as opposed to just memorizing the Word. As well, having the relationship will help them to understand the importance of fellowship with other believers, as well as help them to know that a church is any group of people that gather in fellowship, even if that happens to be in your living room.

So, until our kids have cultivated their relationship with God enough that they can spiritually discern and hear the voice of God within themselves, we rarely let them spend the night at other's homes. This is mostly because even if I know the person very well, I may not know everyone or have met everyone that has access to their home. They could have friends or family members or other kids coming to the sleepover that I have not met before and had the chance to spiritually discern that could be exposing my children to something my child isn't prepared for.

For example, there could be a kid attending the sleepover who comes from a home dealing with a spirit of deception. If I know my child is still struggling with being honest, I want to be cautious regarding them hanging around with other children or people who are dealing with a spirit of deception.

Now, please don't take this that I am against sleepovers. I am NOT against sleepovers, lol. My kids have slept over someone's house on rare occasions with people that I trust and who I know understand my concerns about sleepovers and are willing to accommodate those concerns. In addition, I am a firm believer that every parent has to do what they feel is best. Parenting doesn't come with an instruction manual. So do what you think is best for your family. As I stated earlier, the point of our family doing this is because it is one of the ways that we choose to protect our children's "circle" in which they could be influenced.

Some of the other protective measures we have chosen for our family are that our kids aren't allowed to use social media platforms until we feel they have become spiritually mature enough not to allow social media to influence them negatively. We also do a lot of things together as a family to try and strengthen our family bond so that our kids feel comfortable wanting to bring their friends into our family circle. This way, we get to know their friends, and we want our kids to feel comfortable talking to us about things they are talking to their friends about at school. By no means am I saying this system works perfectly, and that we believe our kids tell us everything. Kids are still kids, but I do feel confident that we have open lines of communication within our family, for the most part. These are just a few things that we do to try and protect our children's "circle" of influence.

In a later chapter, I will talk more in-depth about preventive measures that can help to protect your child from Spiritual influence. The critical point that I would hope everyone reading, to take away from this chapter, is that Spiritual influence can happen and that more than likely, it will occur through your child's circle. So, protect the circle.

* * *

Things to Consider/Actions to Take:

What "gates" (behaviors/habits) do you think your child might currently be struggling with keeping closed so that they don't fall into being spiritually influenced?

How might you be currently negatively influencing your child spiritually? What behaviors/habits may you need to work on stopping, to protect your child better?

Who might you need to consider cutting out of your child's circle, until your child becomes stronger spiritually to protect themselves from that person's negative spiritual influence?

III

Preventive Care- Spiritual Vitamins and Boosting Spiritual Immunity

5

The Medicine Cabinet- The Power of Prayer/God's Word

"...and this is the confidence we have in him, that, if we ask any thing according to his will, he heareth us..."- 1 John 5:14(KJV)

What is Prayer?

Prayer. Usually, when someone mentions the word prayer, there are a few different mental images that come to my mind. I often associate the word with an image of someone's hands together on a bent knee at an altar. Or someone crossed-legged, hands resting on their knees, and palms up in a meditative state. However, the reality is that prayer for me looks like everyday living. That is because prayer for me is really just my conversation with God. I am literally continually praying throughout the day during regular day-to-day tasks. My relationship with God is a friendship, in which He represents so many different positions in my life. I could go on for hours talking to you about my friend God, but that isn't what this book is necessarily about. But maybe in a different book I can talk about that. So, because our relationship works as a friendship, I talk to Him all throughout the day while doing other tasks. The "prayers" are much more conversational, and I talk to Him much like I speak to any of my friends. One of the things I love about this kind of prayer is that sometimes in my very chaotic thought life, God is the peace and voice of reason and wisdom I have come to depend on. Other times He is just my confidant, listening to me ramble to Him, about whatever. This is how I pray the majority of the time. I am sharing this to let you know that prayer doesn't have to be formal. It can be, but it doesn't have to be. The dictionary definition of prayer, according to dictionary.com, has several different meanings. However, the one most noted is defined as "a spiritual communion with God or an object of worship, as in supplication, thanksgiving, adoration, or confession."[1](Dictionary.com) I think most people would agree that prayer, though, is simply communicating with God, or your higher power. What it looks like can be different for each of us, depending on how your relationship with God works. You also don't have to do it the same every time.

For instance, even though I pray throughout the day in conversation with God, I also make time most mornings, where I have a more meditative formal prayer time. That time for me is my alone time with God. I get excited about prayer time. It's my time where I get to give God my undivided attention and spend some quality time with Him. It's also the time more often than not that He really lays down the "meat and potatoes" that have come in my spiritual growth. I believe this is because this is also the time where I am most attentive to listening to Him. I have found that if I make time for God, He makes time to teach and invest in me spiritually.

This more dedicated prayer time for me, has a little more of formal anatomy to it, than my conversational prayer time. It is an anatomy that I have shared with my kids when I first began to teach them how to pray. This was before we got into the depths of teaching them the importance of building a relationship with God. I also like to share it with people who are unsure of how to start a prayer life and are looking for a way to start the conversation with God.

---

[1] "prayer." Dictionary.com. 2020. https://www.dictionary.com (20 July 2020)

* * *

The Anatomy of a Basic Prayer

So even though you can just dive right into a conversation with God, and start a prayer as you see fit, if you want a fundamental place to begin, this is how my more formal prayers are structured.

- Show gratitude
- Pray for others/those in need
- Submit your own worries or concerns
- Leave space to listen

I think showing gratitude is always a great place to start with God. Not only does it bring me great joy to give Him thanks, but I also always find there isn't enough that I can give Him thanks for once I start showing my gratitude. Also, starting my morning with a spirit of gratitude does wonders for my day. It usually gets you in a good place spiritually, that allows God's Holy Spirit to move in you and help guide you through your prayer. This is what we want! We want the Holy Spirit to influence our prayers. No one knows better what is needed in your life or the lives of those you hold dear, than God. So, having the Holy Spirit influence our prayer life is how we can ensure that we are praying for the right things. Showing God gratitude will encourage this influence.

Gratitude can also be expressed via song. Maybe you can't think of the right words, but a song comes to mind or speaks to your spirit. Sing your gratitude! There have been mornings, where God has just laid a spirit of praise over me, and I just want to sing and let Him know how amazing He is to me. Maybe you are like me and also feel compelled to write your praise. Sometimes I feel like God, and I have our best conversations when I am writing to Him.

There was a time in my spiritual journey, where I could only hear God clearly if I were writing. Maybe that is where you are as well. The point here is that gratitude can be expressed in many different ways, so choose which approach works best for you and your relationship with God.

After you are finished expressing gratitude, the next place you can go is to submit your concerns and cares for others to the altar, if you will, of you, and God's bond. This is usually where I submit my prayers for my family, friends, people around the world, issues that are weighing on me for others in the world, and the subject of this book, your kids and their needs. This is the space in which you can bring to God, your child's spiritual health. If you know/or suspect them to be struggling with any type of specific issues of concern, you can ask God to deliver them from those issues are negative spirits. When I am asking God to help heal them, I usually find that my prayers naturally transition into me, asking God to give myself guidance on how to help them as well.

Since God has allowed us to be a partner with Him in raising His children, as parents, we ultimately want to make sure we are in alignment with His Will for them. This is why the next place in a prayer is to naturally lead into our own personal concerns and request from God. Generally, for me, those concerns start with how I can be of better service as a mother, friend, servant of God, wife, or family member. It can also lead to me asking God to help me grow in areas where I feel weak or asking for strength to endure, or as a mom, if I am honest, a lot of times, I am asking God for PATIENCE! (lol, but true) Yet, as I begin laying all of my concerns on the table for myself or my children, sometimes God and I begin to have a conversation. When I say a conversation, I do mean a back and forth conversation. I say this only because I remember a time in my own spiritual journey when others would speak about conversing with God, and I didn't understand how that worked since I was not yet at that place. Even now, my own kids question me constantly on how they can talk to God because when they try, they don't feel like he is responding. If you are a person like this, what I would say to you is God speaks to each of us in many different ways. Sometimes it can be directly through prayer and meditation. Sometimes it is through an experience. Sometimes it can be through another person, and sometimes as I have found in recent years, He can speak to you through your own children, without them even knowing. For myself, it doesn't happen the same way all the time; this is why I said, "sometimes, we began to conversate." Nonetheless, start the conversation with Him and then leave space for Him to answer.

The space where God can answer doesn't always happen at the end of the prayer; however, I still like to end my prayer time trying to be mentally and spiritually silent and listening. Most of us who do pray, tend to spend a lot of time talking to God, and maybe not enough time listening or just in silence with Him. Sometimes that may be because we struggle to be mentally and spiritually silent, or we may not feel like we have enough time. Yet, I think it is important that we try to give God this time at the end of prayer because if we are good friends to God, we should share this space of prayer and let Him have the opportunity to speak in the moment if He chooses. Remember, prayer is supposed to be a conversation between you and God, and in regards to your kids you are co-parenting, so even more so when it comes to your child's spiritual health give God the opportunity to speak.

* * *

The Word-Your Spiritual Vitamins

Earlier I discussed a couple of different ways in which God may speak to you. However, the one I didn't mention is through His Word. The Bible contains many of the answers we seek from God, right within its pages. In my spiritual journey, the Bible has become not only a way for God to communicate with me but also a place of refuge, encouragement, peace, and, most importantly, a foundation for me to stand on against the enemy. In terms of thinking about my spiritual health, I would compare the Bible to a medicine cabinet of spiritual vitamins, if you will, where I can go and eat from when I feel deficient in a specific area. There are usually several places to find verses that can help you with your spiritual ailment. (I have included a list of verses at the end of this book)

For instance, when I am feeling anxious, two places I can go to are Philippians 4:7 and 1 Peter 5:7. When I am feeling spiritually weak, I can turn to 2 Corinthians 12:9 or Isaiah 40:31. These are just a few examples of verses I use as spiritual vitamins to feed me when I am feeling deficient. God tells us to eat from his "daily bread." Food is known for being medicine for the body, and I believe the "daily bread" is food for our spirits. God knew we would need this "medicine" daily for our spiritual "bodies." So we should use His Word as manna, and not let it go to waste!

For me, I like to meditate on these verses when I am looking for a change in spirit. I read the verses as if they are affirmations, daily, or as needed. The Bible serves as a foundation that I feel comfortable standing on in the face of doubt. This is also what I try to teach my children. I want them to understand that when they feel like they are struggling with their own doubts about themselves or God, they can turn to the Word as a foundation, in addition to prayer.

* * *

Warrior Mode-Fighting A Virus

"Is any sick among you? Let him call for the elders of the church; and let them pray over him, anointing him with oil in the name of the Lord: And the prayer of faith

shall save the sick, and the Lord shall raise him up; and if he have committed sins,
they shall be forgiven him. Confess your faults one to another, and pray one for
another, that ye may be healed. The effectual fervent prayer of a righteous man
availeth much."-James 5:14-16 (KJV)

Now that we have talked about prayer, and the Word and how they serve you in your spiritual medicine cabinet, now I want to talk to you about the POWER in using these things to fight against spiritual attacks.

In my everyday life, and in my husband and I's efforts to work toward safeguarding our children's spiritual health, things are pretty peaceful for the most part. I feel like as a family we have laid down a pretty good spiritual foundation in our household, that most times when we need to address any issues or concerns spiritually, we know what routines to put in motion to fight against them. My kids even know what to do in most cases, without having to ask me for help. As they have gotten older, my daughter has had more questions about God answering her when she prays, but for the most part, they know the basics. However, there are times when the regular routines we have in place aren't enough. It could be because we have gotten distracted and not made time for God. It could be we have neglected our kids' needs because we ourselves have been dealing with something, and that has been a distraction. Whatever the case may be, there are times when we come under a significant spiritual attack, and when we notice it, it is time for us to go into spiritual warrior mode.

I would relate these times to be similar to your body coming under an infectious attack and your White blood cells having to gear up and go to war to protect the body wherever there's an infection. Even though white blood cells only make up a tiny percentage of our blood, they are pretty powerful in defending our bodies. They are always at war with bacteria and other harmful things in our bodies. However, when the body comes under attack in a specific area, they can rush in and do some severe damage to defend our bodies from the intruders. For me, this is similar to what going into spiritual warrior mode looks like. Tapping into the power that God has given us through prayer and His word, through the blood of Jesus, to stand against the enemy and any other negative force that would try and come against us.

When the enemy tries to attack us, the Bible tells us to,
"Put on the whole armour of God, that ye may be able to stand against the wiles of the devil."- Ephesians 6:11 (KJV)
What is the full armour of God? The Bible tells us that the whole armor of God includes:
"...with the belt of truth buckled around your waist, with the breastplate of righteousness in place, and with your feet fitted with the readiness that comes from the gospel of peace. In addition to all of this, take up the shield of faith, with which you can extinguish all the flaming arrows of the evil one. Take the helmet of salvation and the sword of the Spirit, which is the word of God." - Ephesians 6:14-17 (NIV)
From this passage, we can understand that the armor consists of:

- A belt of truth
- A breastplate of righteousness
- A Shield of Faith
- A helmet of Salvation
- A sword consisting of the Spirit or Word of God

Truth, Righteousness, Faith, Salvation, and the Word of God are what make up our spiritual white blood cells. We strengthen our ability to use these spiritual white blood cells by feeding them through prayer and God's word. Just like we strengthen our bodies, white blood cells by feeding ourselves the proper nutrition and boosting them with vitamins.

When I go into warrior mode, I truly step into the power that God has given us to overcome the enemy's attacks. We are made powerful through these pillars that make up our spiritual white blood cells. Through the blessing of our Salvation and our Faith in God, we can stand in the Truths of God's word to come against any attack. Jesus said:

"Behold, I give unto you power to tread on serpents and scorpions, and over all the power of the enemy: and nothing shall by any means hurt you."- Luke 10:19 (KJV)

You have the authority to overcome ALL the power of the enemy. Stand in that truth, and own it. That is POWER. There is power in God's word, and this verse right here alone, is an example of that power. There is power in prayer. God's word tells us:

"The righteous cry and the Lord heareth, and delivereth them out of all their troubles." -Psalms 34:17 (KJV)

All their troubles, it says. Not some, but all. This is the power that comes from praying to our God and submitting to His Will. These are some of the verses I lean on when I need to go into warrior mode prayer. They become affirmations for me in fighting against whatever is trying to attack our family.

When we need to go into warrior mode, my husband and I will even make a point to get up early and start to pray together. Sometimes we even walk through our home reciting Psalms 91 and singing praises to God. These aren't things that we do regularly. He and I have different places and ways in which we hear from God. My husband has his best moments with God while he is at the gym. In comparison, I have my best moments while either journaling or during morning meditation. So usually, we are praying separately. Yet, when we take notice of spiritual attacks, we come together and join forces. Jesus says in Matthew:

"Again I say unto you, That if two of you shall agree on earth as touching any thing that they shall ask, it shall be done for them of my Father which is in heaven. For where two or three are gathered together in my name, there am I in the midst of them." -Matthew 18:19-20 (KJV)

Again, this is the kind of power we have to overcome spiritual attacks when we pray. I think it is always better to have someone that can pray with you when you need to go into warrior mode. If you have a spouse, that is even better. I have heard it said before that when a husband and wife come together in prayer, it is truly a powerful thing. I believe it is because God has blessed that union, and maybe God even more so honors their prayers.

In conclusion, what I think is most important to take from this section, is that it is essential to build a relationship with God through prayer and to have regular digestion of God's word, for both you and your child. This is because doing so will strengthen the pillars of your spiritual white blood cells, to prepare your family to be ready if you ever need to go into warrior mode defense against a spiritual attack.

* * *

<u>Things to Consider/Actions to Take:</u>

In an effort to work on building a relationship with God, what time can you designate each week to have alone time with God? (i.e., on your commute, before bed, on a lunch break)

To help your child have a better understanding of how to pray, what time can you designate to practice prayer with your child? (i.e., at dinner, at bedtime)

Are there any areas in either you or your child's spiritual health, that you think may be suffering from deficiencies? If so, find a couple of scriptures to speak as affirmations this week, to help supplement those areas of weakness. (There is a list of scriptures at the end of this book on page 52. Also, I love the "Bible" App to help with this. They make it very easy to locate scriptures based on areas of concern.)

6

Teaching Good "Spiritual Health" Habits

"Train up a child in the way he should go: and when he is old, he will not depart from it." -Proverbs 22:6 (KJV)

Helping your child to learn good spiritual health habits will benefit them, much like teaching good hygiene does. Learning them will help reduce the risk of spreading spiritual germs and getting spiritually sick. Establishing a good prayer foundation and allowing your kids to study the word is just as beneficial for their spiritual health, as learning how to wash their hands properly and eating their veggies is for their physical health.

Teaching your Child to Pray

Now that we have talked about what prayer is, and the anatomy of a basic prayer, the next thing I would like to discuss is how to establish a foundation of prayer in your child's life. Since I am no expert on the child psyche, nor do I have a degree in childhood development, I can only speak to you on this from experience as a mother. In this section, I am going to share with you how we started our kids out in prayer and how we progressed them in prayer as they have gotten older. (My kids are now 13 and 10, as I write this.)

We started our kids out with praying over food and before bed before they could even speak very well. I would say a "nursery prayer" that I learned as a kid with them, at these times, so that they got used to the action being done. Toddlers do a lot of mimicking, so they would try to mimic along until, eventually, they were able to memorize and recite the prayers on their own. Finally, they got to a place where they would do this without prompt. (You can find examples of these "nursery prayers" in the next chapter on page 64) These prayers were their go-to prayers until they were about 6 or 7 yrs old.

Once our kids reached grade school age, we begin to add on to their prayer life. One thing we added was asking them before bed if there were anyone that they would like to pray for or anything they would like to ask God to help them with. We would talk about how God can help them and others. We also discussed how He listens to prayers and why it was important to pray because God wants us to talk to Him and be His friend. This is the age where we try to help our kids understand that God is more than just some God in the sky. We wanted them to begin to realize that God can be more personal than that.

Another thing we introduced at this age is home bible study. We had already had picture bibles that they looked at, or we read when they were toddlers. At this age, though, we want to start more of a discussion with them about the bible. The kids are now in grade school doing assignments, so I think this is a good age for them also to start a basic studying of the Word. For us, this wasn't something we did regularly (unless we saw the kids struggling with something particular that required more attention to the Word). This was just something we did on occasion as a family so that the kids could start the habit of reading the Word, thinking, and answering questions about it. During these Bible studies, we would also end it with prayer. I asked the kids just to pray and say whatever was on their hearts. At this age, I didn't try and correct them or give guidance unless they asked. I just let them pray whatever they wanted. Sometimes the stuff they would say would be the silliest things, and sometimes they would completely shock me in knowing what I needed prayer for at that time. (This also encouraged me in knowing that they were unknowingly hearing and being influenced by the Holy Spirit) I didn't care as much about what they prayed for, as much as I just wanted them to begin feeling comfortable speaking from their heart to God.

When my kids reached the ages of 8 and 9, this is when we introduced the basic anatomy of a prayer. At this age, we begin talking more about what it meant to be a friend to God. We also began to talk more about hearing from God. These questions seemed to naturally come up as we talked about scripture over the years, and as we prayed as a family when they were dealing with issues of concern. So, as their spiritual maturity grew, so did their prayer life. They wanted to know more about praying on their own. So it seems like this was the natural age to introduce the basic anatomy of prayer, as well as talk more about showing gratitude. This is also the age when we begin dissecting the Word more. I found an excellent guide sheet on Pinterest to help them walk through scripture in a kid-friendly way. This allowed us to dig in more thoughtfully to the Word.

Once my kids reached preteen years, their prayers were a lot more thoughtful and discerning. At the ages of 10-13, I must boast here that I feel incredibly proud of where my kids are spiritually. I know they aren't perfect, but I am grateful for their spiritual maturity and journey. I can see that they both have their own relationships with God and that they seek Him on their own. When my son prays, I feel the spirit of God in His prayers. My daughter, who is ten right now, still struggles sometimes with praying, and I know that it is because she is in a place of curiosity and doubt about her and God's relationship. I still feel proud of this because I know she is seeking Him and looking for answers. She asks me questions all the time about how she can better hear God. She talks to me about how she keeps working to be a better person, that God would be happy with. These kinds of conversations make me proud because I know that she is trying to build a relationship with God. When we have these discussions, I try to ease her worries by reminding her that I am almost 40 yrs old and still working on some of the things she is talking about. This is to help her put in perspective that she has time to get it right. I remind her that I didn't even hear God's voice for myself until I was in college. I remind her that God answers us in different ways, and I give her examples of ways God has already responded to her, but she may not have recognized. I remind her that the important part at her age is that she builds a personal relationship with God by praying and reading the Word.

Also, at this age, I have invited my kids into my own prayer/meditation time in the mornings on occasion. I did this so that my kids could see what my alone time with God looks like. I also wanted them to see how simple showing gratitude can be. Kids sometimes struggle with showing gratitude, at least mine do! I feel like we live in a time when many kids, and adults for that matter, feel entitled. With that in mind, I can see why some people struggle with understanding how simple showing gratitude can be. For me showing gratitude can be as simple as thanking God for the relationship he has with us, thanking Him for the moment alone with Him, and thanking Him for the right mind to form this sentence. I want my kids to understand this kind of gratitude. Yet, when they live in a time where so many of their peers feel entitled to everything, I get why understanding what to show gratitude for can sometimes be a struggle.

If you are a parent who hasn't established the foundation we did early, maybe inviting your child to take the spiritual journey with you is where you start. I don't think it is too late to build a foundation, even if your kids are older. If they still live with you and are under your responsibility, then start this journey with them.

* * *

Sneaking in "Spiritual Veggies"

We talked in the previous chapter about how the Word works like vitamins for your spiritual health. Vitamins usually come naturally from veggies; however, most kids don't like eating vegetables when they are young. The same can be said about trying to get your kid to read the Word. Most of the bible isn't always kid-friendly in reading subjects. So in this section, I want to talk about some different ways to make learning and reading from the Word more kid-friendly at home.

So one of the easiest ways to start introducing the Word to your child as a toddler is through picture Bibles. There are a lot of kid-friendly bibles on the market to choose from. I have listed the name of the bible we used when our kids were toddlers, in the "Additional Resources" section. This is pretty much the extent of what we did when our kids were toddlers in regards to sharing the Word with them. We used that Bible during storytime sometimes, and let the kids read along.

Once your kids hit grade school age, you can introduce a couple of other resources. For us, we got them kid study bibles, and we would use them when we had bible study at home. We also bought them a kids' devotional book. We would let them read and talk about what they thought about the scripture or devotionals. I spoke in an earlier chapter, about how when the kids were struggling with a specific area, we would use a list of scriptures on that topic. This is another way that gets them familiar with the Word. I would have the kids pick a scripture from the list that they would have to memorize and tell me how they could apply it to their life. We would also go through the list of scriptures dealing with the issue of concern, every night, reading them and talking about whether they were able to apply any of them to their life that day specifically.

A more game-friendly way that we introduced the Word was using bible flash cards. So we found some flashcards with bible trivia questions on them in both easy or hard categories. (listed on page 65) As a family at dinner time, we started using the flashcards to test what we knew about the bible. The winner was whoever had the most cards at the end. There usually was no prize other than bragging rights, but the kids still enjoy doing this even now. Another fun activity once my kids reached preteen age, is letting them be the teacher of at-home bible study. I let them pick the scripture and lead the discussion. They enjoy being in charge of the lesson.

Overall, the kids enjoy the trivia game the most because they don't always initially enjoy having to put down their games or electronics to have bible study. However, by the end of the lesson, they are usually happy that we did it, and on the rare occasion, I even get them asking me when we will do it again! So, even if your adolescent or preteen groans about having to "eat their spiritual veggies," they need it, so bare through the groans.

* * *

Things to Consider/Actions to Take:

Reflecting on the examples I gave, when and how will you start introducing prayer into your child's life regularly?

If you are looking for a way to start introducing scripture to your child, maybe start with the Lord's prayer. Or do you have a favorite piece of scripture that you would like to share with your child?

Can you think of a way to make learning a piece of scripture fun for your child?

IV

Stocking Your Medicine Cabinet & Disinfecting Your Home

7

Scriptures and Prayers to Cover Your Home and Family-Parents

The following pages in this section are a collection of scriptures and prayers that I thought would be nice to share, for any parent's struggling to either find their way or looking for resources to begin. I hope you find them helpful!

Scriptures to reference by issue of concern:

Quick Reference Chart below, King James Version of scriptures available after chart.

Protection	Encouragement	Obedience	Strength
Psalm 91	2 Corinthians 4:16	Psalm 139:23-24	2 Corinthians 12:9
Proverbs 18:10	Psalms 34:8	1 Kings 3:14	1 Peter 5:10
Ephesians 6:13-18	James 1:2-4	2 John 1:6	2 Corinthians 4:16-18
Matthew 6:9-13	Romans 3:23-25	Deuteronomy 5:33	Philippians 4:13
2 Samuel 22:2-3	Jeremiah 29:11	Jeremiah 7:23	Isaiah 40:29
Entitlement/Gratitude	Deception/Honesty	Pride/Humility	Compassion/Love
Romans 2:4	John 4:24	Mark 10:43-45	1 Corinthians 13:4-7
Colossians 3:16	Proverbs 12:22	Ephesians 2:8-10	Luke 6:32-36
1 Thessalonians 5:18	Hebrews 13:18	Psalms 36:2	1 John 4:7-8
James 1:17	Psalm 52:2	Philippians 2:3	Romans 12:10
Colossians 3:17	Exodus 20:16	James 4:10	Matthew 5:44
Fear	Peace	Healing	Worry
2 Timothy 1:7	Philippians 4:7	Mark 5:34	Philippians 4:6
1 John 4:18	John 16:33	James 5:14-16	Matthew 6:25-27
Psalms 56:3	2 Thessalonians 3:16	Psalms 103:2-3	Matthew 6:34
Psalms 34:4	Isaiah 26:3	Jeremiah 33:6	1 Peter 5:7
Joshua 1:9	John 14:27	Isaiah 58:8	Matthew 6:31

Protection:

He that dwelleth in the secret place of the most High shall abide under the shadow of the Almighty. I will say of the Lord, He is my refuge and my fortress: my God; in him will I trust. Surely he shall deliver thee from the snare of the fowler, and from the noisome pestilence. He shall cover thee with his feathers, and under his wings shalt thou trust: his truth shall be thy shield and buckler. Thou shalt not be afraid for the terror by night; nor for the arrow that flieth by day; Nor for the pestilence that walketh in darkness; nor for the destruction that wasteth at noonday. A thousand shall fall at thy side, and ten thousand at thy right hand; but it shall not come nigh thee. Only with thine eyes shalt thou behold and see the reward of the wicked. Because thou hast made the Lord, which is my refuge, even the most High, thy habitation; There shall no evil befall thee, neither shall any plague come nigh thy dwelling. For he shall give his angels charge over thee, to keep thee in all thy ways. They shall bear thee up in their hands, lest thou dash thy foot against a stone. Thou shalt tread upon the lion and adder: the young lion and the dragon shalt thou trample under feet. Because he hath set his love upon me, therefore will I deliver him: I will set him on high, because he hath known my name. He shall call upon me, and I will answer him: I will be with him in trouble; I will deliver him, and honour him. With long life will I satisfy him, and shew him my salvation. -Psalm 91:1-16

The name of the Lord is a strong tower: the righteous runneth into it, and is safe. -Proverbs 18:10

Wherefore take unto you the whole armour of God, that ye may be able to withstand in the evil day, and having done all, to stand. Stand therefore, having your loins girt about with truth, and having on the breastplate of righteousness; And your feet shod with the preparation of the gospel of peace; Above all, taking the shield of faith, wherewith ye shall be able to quench all the fiery darts of the wicked. And take the helmet of salvation, and the sword of the Spirit, which is the word of God: Praying always with all prayer and supplication in the Spirit, and watching thereunto with all perseverance and supplication for all saints; - Ephesians 6:13-18 After this manner therefore pray ye: Our Father which art in heaven, Hallowed be thy name. Thy kingdom come. Thy will be done on earth, as it is in heaven. Give us this day our daily bread. And forgive us our debts, as we forgive our debtors. And lead us not into temptation, but deliver us from evil: For thine is the kingdom, and the power, and the glory, for ever. Amen. -Matthew 6:9-13

And he said, The Lord is my rock, and my fortress, and my deliverer; The God of my rock; in him will I trust: he is my shield, and the horn of my salvation, my high tower, and my refuge, my saviour; thou savest me from violence. -2 Samuel 22:2-3

Encouragement:
For which cause we faint not; but though our outward man perishes, yet the inward man is renewed day by day. -2 Corinthians 4:16

O taste and see that the Lord is good: blessed is the man that trusteth in him.
-Psalms 34:8

My brethren, count it all joy when ye fall into divers temptations; Knowing this, that the trying of your faith worketh patience. But let patience have her perfect work, that ye may be perfect and entire, wanting nothing. -James 1:2-4

For all have sinned, and come short of the glory of God; Being justified freely by his grace through the redemption that is in Christ Jesus: Whom God hath set forth to be a propitiation through faith in his blood, to declare his righteousness for the remission of sins that are past, through the forbearance of God; -Romans 3:23-25

For I know the thoughts that I think toward you, saith the Lord, thoughts of peace, and not of evil, to give you an expected end. -Jeremiah 29:11

Obedience:

Search me, O God, and know my heart: try me, and know my thoughts: And see if there be any wicked way in me, and lead me in the way everlasting. -Psalms 139:23-24

And if thou wilt walk in my ways, to keep my statutes and my commandments, as thy father David did walk, then I will lengthen thy days. -1 Kings 3:14

And this is love, that we walk after his commandments. This is the commandment, That, as ye have heard from the beginning, ye should walk in it. -2 John 1:6

Ye shall walk in all the ways which the Lord your God hath commanded you, that ye may live, and that it may be well with you, and that ye may prolong your days in the land which ye shall possess. - Deuteronomy 5:33

But this thing commanded I them, saying, Obey my voice, and I will be your God, and ye shall be my people: and walk ye in all the ways that I have commanded you, that it may be well unto you. - Jeremiah 7:23

Strength:

And he said unto me, My grace is sufficient for thee: for my strength is made perfect in weakness. Most gladly therefore will I rather glory in my infirmities, that the power of Christ may rest upon me. -2 Corinthians 12:9

But the God of all grace, who hath called us unto his eternal glory by Christ Jesus, after that ye have suffered a while, make you perfect, stablish, strengthen, settle you.
-1 Peter 5:10

For which cause we faint not; but though our outward man perish, yet the inward man is renewed day by day. For our light affliction, which is but for a moment, worketh for us a far more exceeding and eternal weight of glory; While we look not at the things which are seen, but at the things which are not seen: for the things which are seen are temporal; but the things which are not seen are eternal. -2 Corinthians 4:16-18

I can do all things through Christ which strengtheneth me. -Philippians 4:13
He giveth power to the faint; and to them that have no might he increaseth strength.

-Isaiah 40:29

Entitlement/Gratitude:

Or despisest thou the riches of his goodness and forbearance and longsuffering; not knowing that the goodness of God leadeth thee to repentance? -Romans 2:4

Let the word of Christ dwell in you richly in all wisdom; teaching and admonishing one another in psalms and hymns and spiritual songs, singing with grace in your hearts to the Lord.
-Colossians 3:16

In every thing give thanks: for this is the will of God in Christ Jesus concerning you.
-1 Thessalonians 5:18

Every good gift and every perfect gift is from above, and cometh down from the Father of lights, with whom is no variableness, neither shadow of turning. -James 1:17

And whatsoever ye do in word or deed, do all in the name of the Lord Jesus, giving thanks to God and the Father by him. -Colossians 3:17

Deception/Honesty:
God is a Spirit: and they that worship him must worship him in spirit and in truth. -John 4:24

Lying lips are abomination to the Lord: but they that deal truly are his delight. -Proverbs 12:22

*Pray for us: for we trust we have a good conscience, in all things willing to live honestly.
-Hebrews 13:18*

Thy tongue deviseth mischiefs; like a sharp razor, working deceitfully. -Psalms 52:2

Thou shalt not bear false witness against thy neighbour. -Exodus 20:16

Pride/Humility:
But so shall it not be among you: but whosoever will be great among you, shall be your minister: And whosoever of you will be the chiefest, shall be servant of all. For even the Son of man came not to be ministered unto, but to minister, and to give his life a ransom for many. -Mark 10:43-45

For by grace are ye saved through faith; and that not of yourselves: it is the gift of God: Not of works, lest any man should boast. For we are his workmanship, created in Christ Jesus unto good works, which God hath before ordained that we should walk in them. -Ephesians 2:8-10

For he flattereth himself in his own eyes, until his iniquity be found to be hateful.
-Psalms 36:2

Let nothing be done through strife or vainglory; but in lowliness of mind let each
esteem other better than themselves. -Philippians 2:3

Humble yourselves in the sight of the Lord, and he shall lift you up. -James 4:10

Compassion/Love:

Charity suffereth long, and is kind; charity envieth not; charity vaunteth not itself,
is not puffed up, Doth not behave itself unseemly, seeketh not her own, is not easily
provoked, thinketh no evil; Rejoiceth not in iniquity, but rejoiceth in the truth;
Beareth all things, believeth all things, hopeth all things, endureth all things. -1
Corinthians 13:4-7

For if ye love them which love you, what thank have ye? for sinners also love those
that love them. And if ye do good to them which do good to you, what thank have
ye? for sinners also do even the same. And if ye lend to them of whom ye hope to
receive, what thank have ye? for sinners also lend to sinners, to receive as much
again. But love ye your enemies, and do good, and lend, hoping for nothing again;
and your reward shall be great, and ye shall be the children of the Highest: for he is
kind unto the unthankful and to the evil. Be ye therefore merciful, as your Father
also is merciful. -Luke 6:32-36

Beloved, let us love one another: for love is of God; and every one that loveth is
born of God, and knoweth God. He that loveth not knoweth not God; for God is
love. -1 John 4:7-8

Be kindly affectioned one to another with brotherly love; in honour preferring one
another -Romans 12:10

But I say unto you, Love your enemies, bless them that curse you, do good to them
that hate you, and pray for them which despitefully use you, and persecute you

55

-Matthew 5:44

Fear:

For God hath not given us the spirit of fear; but of power, and of love, and of a sound mind.
-2 Timothy 1:7

There is no fear in love; but perfect love casteth out fear: because fear hath torment. He that feareth is not made perfect in love. -1 John 4:18

What time I am afraid, I will trust in thee. -Psalms 56:3

I sought the Lord, and he heard me, and delivered me from all my fears. -Psalms 34:4

Have not I commanded thee? Be strong and of a good courage; be not afraid, neither be thou dismayed: for the Lord thy God is with thee whithersoever thou goest. -Joshua 1:9

Peace:

And the peace of God, which passeth all understanding, shall keep your hearts and minds through Christ Jesus. -Philippians 4:7

These things I have spoken unto you, that in me ye might have peace. In the world ye shall have tribulation: but be of good cheer; I have overcome the world. -John 16:33

Now the Lord of peace himself give you peace always by all means. The Lord be with you all.
-2 Thessolonians 3:16

Thou wilt keep him in perfect peace, whose mind is stayed on thee: because he trusteth in thee.

-Isaiah 26:3

Peace I leave with you, my peace I give unto you: not as the world giveth, give I unto you. Let not your heart be troubled, neither let it be afraid. -John 14:27

Healing:

And he said unto her, Daughter, thy faith hath made thee whole; go in peace, and be whole of thy plague. -Mark 5:34

Is any sick among you? let him call for the elders of the church; and let them pray over him, anointing him with oil in the name of the Lord: And the prayer of faith shall save the sick, and the Lord shall raise him up; and if he have committed sins, they shall be forgiven him. Confess your faults one to another, and pray one for another, that ye may be healed. The effectual fervent prayer of a righteous man availeth much. -James 5:14-16

Bless the Lord, O my soul, and forget not all his benefits: Who forgiveth all thine iniquities; who healeth all thy diseases -Psalms 103:2-3

Behold, I will bring it health and cure, and I will cure them, and will reveal unto them the abundance of peace and truth. -Jeremiah 33:6

*Then shall thy light break forth as the morning, and thine health shall spring forth speedily: and thy righteousness shall go before thee; the glory of the Lord shall be thy rearward.
-Isaiah 58:8*

Worry:

Be careful for nothing; but in every thing by prayer and supplication with thanksgiving let your requests be made known unto God. -Philippians 4:6

Therefore I say unto you, Take no thought for your life, what ye shall eat, or what ye shall drink; nor yet for your body, what ye shall put on. Is not the life more than meat, and the body than raiment? Behold the fowls of the air: for they sow not, neither do they reap, nor gather into barns; yet your heavenly Father feedeth them. Are ye not much better than they? Which of you by taking thought can add one cubit unto his stature? -Matthew 6:25-27

Take therefore no thought for the morrow: for the morrow shall take thought for the things of itself. Sufficient unto the day is the evil thereof. -Matthew 6:34

Therefore take no thought, saying, What shall we eat? or, What shall we drink? or, Wherewithal shall we be clothed? -Matthew 6:31

Casting all your care upon him; for he careth for you. -1 Peter 5:7

8

Prayers for You and Your Family

I think it is essential to stock your "medicine cabinet" with a variety of easily accessible resources. For my family, we have been gifted a few books of prayers that I like to use when I am struggling with what to pray about. Below I will provide a few examples of prayers that I love for various situations; however, I want also to share the resources that I have found helpful from other authors.

The first that I would like to share is a book called "The Little Red Prayer Book." It is by Christian Word Ministries, located in Kentucky. If you go to their website, they now offer an e-book that you can download for free. (Website: www.christianword.org) They offer all different kinds of prayers for many different situations. They even provide prayers specifically for children and teens.

Another great resource that I like to utilize is a book titled "Prayers That Avail Much" by Germaine Copeland. This book also has a great variety of prayers for different occasions. One of the things I love about this book is that it includes scriptures that accompany each prayer.

Both of these books have sections that deal specifically with praying over your children/teens. I hope that you would take the time to look into these resources to add to what I provide in the following section. They have been much appreciated through my spiritual walk as places to turn to when I felt at a loss on what to pray.

Nonetheless, to hopefully be a place to start right away, the following are a few of my personal go-to prayers for different occasions.

Prayer of Protection

Whenever I feel like myself, or my family has come under spiritual attack, I like to walk through my house reading Psalms 91 as a prayer. This is one of my favorite prayers of protection. It is an excellent reminder of how great of a shepherd God is to us. I have also used this prayer when we move into a new space/ home. My husband and I, when we feel our family is under attack, will make a point to wake up early and walk the house praying this Psalms together. Going in and out of every room reciting this prayer, and it brings us peace. So, I hope you find as much use and love for this Psalms as my family has.

Psalms 91:

"Whoever dwells in the shelter of the Most High will rest in the shadow of the Almighty. I will say of the Lord, "He is my refuge and my fortress, my God, in whom I trust." Surely he will save you from the fowler's snare and from the deadly pestilence. He will cover you with his feathers, and under his wings you will find refuge; his faithfulness will be your shield and rampart. You will not fear the terror of night, nor the arrow that flies by day, nor the pestilence that stalks in the darkness, nor the plague that destroys at midday. A thousand may fall at your side, ten thousand at your right hand, but it will not come near you. You will only observe with your eyes and see the punishment of the wicked. If you say, "The Lord is my refuge," and you make the Most High your dwelling, no harm will overtake you, no disaster will come near your tent. For he will command his angels concerning you to guard you in all your ways; they will lift you up in their hands, so that you will not strike your foot against a stone. You will tread on the lion and the cobra; you will trample the great lion and the serpent. "Because he loves me," says the Lord, "I will rescue him; I will protect him, for he acknowledges my name. He will call on me, and I will answer him; I will be with him in trouble, I will deliver him and honor him. With a long life I will satisfy him and show him my salvation."

Prayer of Peace

One of the things I find myself praying for more than anything is peace. Peace within your spirit can make all the world of difference within not only a parent but also a child. Sometimes my daughter stresses herself to no end trying to make decisions or thinking about the issues of the world. She is a very empathetic child, and she feels deeply for others. I have found myself on many occasions praying that God would comfort her with His Spirit of Peace.

Also, as a mom that still struggles with being patient, I find myself almost hourly, asking God to be my peace! Lord knows I wouldn't make it in this parenting game if it weren't for His Holy Spirit being my peace.

So if you find yourself struggling, or someone you know struggling to find peace within, here is a prayer I would like to share.

Spirit of Peace Prayer:

"Lord, thank you for this moment right now with you. Thank you for the access to Your Holy Spirit. I come right now asking that you would please send your Holy Spirit to comfort (me/or child) during this time of unrest within (my/their) spirit. I pray that (I/they) will find the comfort within you that only you can provide. I pray that your Spirit of Peace would ease (my/their) mind and (my/their) heart, right now, in the name of our Savior Jesus Christ. I thank you in advance for the comfort that I know is coming.

And I find rest in your promises that if we call upon you, you will hear our prayers and come to our aide. I love you, Lord, and thank you for your unwavering Grace, Love, and for the peace that you are bringing. In Jesus' name, I pray, Amen."

Prayer for Wisdom

Also, as a parent, one of the things we may seek often, is the wisdom of God, in knowing how to meet our children's needs best. Parenting doesn't come with a manual, and we are all figuring this thing out as we go. In addition, kids are constantly faced with tough decisions that are both a reflection of their character and shapers of their characters.

I pray regularly that God not only blesses me with the wisdom to guide His children along the right path but that he also would bless them with the wisdom to make wise decisions when I am not around or when dealing with their friends.

If you also have ever struggled with finding wisdom in parenting or in general, I hope these prayers for wisdom will be of help to you.

Prayer for Wisdom in Parenting

"God, thank you so much for the Grace that you provide me in figuring out this here thing called life. I truly appreciate your patience in dealing with me through this journey of life. I pray that right now, you would grant me the wisdom needed to make wise decisions in dealing with your child that you have called me to parent. Grant me the peace within, that I may be able to hear your voice clearly. I pray that you would think through my mind and speak through my lips as I approach this area in which I am seeking your wisdom. Help me to make the best decision that is in accordance with your Will, and I pray that nothing and no one would intervene in your Will being done. Thank you in advance for the Wisdom that you are granting me. In

Jesus' name, I pray. Amen."

Prayer for Wisdom

"God, thank you for this day, and the ability to come to you in prayer. I am coming to you today seeking your wisdom for (myself/ or child), so that (I/she/he) might ensure that (I/she/he) am moving within your Will. Help (me/her/him) to choose wisely in (my/their) interactions and speak wisely in (my/their) conversations, that (I/she/he) may be a good representation of your love to those around (me/her/him). Let your Holy Spirit move within (me/her/him) that (I/she/he) might be guided in accordance with your Will. In Jesus's name, I pray. Amen."

9

Prayers for Kids

This next section will cover a few prayers that you can use to get your toddlers, or young children started in prayer—a few simple prayers for mealtime, bedtime, or just to Give God thanks.

Meal Time prayer (suitable for toddlers)

"God is good; God is great. Thank you for this food that I am about to eat. Amen"

Graduated version

"God is good, God is great, thank you, God, for this food that I am about to eat. Please let it be nourishment of my body, and thank you for the hands that made it. In Jesus's name, I pray, Amen."

Bed Time Prayer (suitable for toddlers)

"Lord that lay me down to sleep, I pray the Lord, my soul, to keep. Please forgive me for all my sins. Amen."

Graduated Version

"Lord that lay me down to sleep, I pray the Lord, my soul, to keep, If I die before I wake, I pray the Lord my soul to take. Thank you, God, for all my family and friends, and please forgive me for all my sins. In Jesus' name Amen."

Prayer for family and friends (suitable for toddlers)

"Thank you, God, for my family and friends, please keep them within your Will. Amen"

Graduated Version

"Thank you, God, for my family and friends, please keep them protected from harm's way, in accordance with Your Will. Thank you, God, for your love and kindness, and for being my friend. Amen"

10

List of Spiritual Songs

B elow is a list of the songs and artists' versions that we like to use when we sing songs of praise. I would like to note that we usually sing the hooks of these songs on repeat when we sing them. It is much easier for kids to learn a hook of a song, as opposed to the entire song, in my own experience. However, there are some songs that I sing in entirety, such as "I Love You," "Jesus Loves Me." and "Hallelujah, Salvation, and Glory." I hope your family finds joy in singing these as we have over the years.

(Note: all of these songs can be found on Spotify unless otherwise noted)

Song List:

Title: "I Love You Lord Today"
   Artist: Maranatha! Gospel

Title: "Hallelujah, Salvation, and Glory"
   Artist: United Voices Choir w/ Stephen Hurd
   (can be found on YouTube)

Title: "He Reigns/Awesome God"
   Artist: Kirk Franklin

Title: "Speak to My Heart"
  Artist: Donnie McClurkin

Title: "Jesus Loves Me"
  Artist: Whitney Houston

11

Additional Resources

I thought I would use this section to share some additional resources that I have found helpful throughout the years. These are items or tools that others have written or come up with, that I have come across on my own journey. Enjoy!

Amazon Finds

- Bible Trivia Christian 50-Count Game Cards (I'm Learning the Bible Flash Cards)- by Twin Sisters (*great family time activity*)
- Scripture Memory Christian 50-Count Game Cards (I'm Learning the Bible Flash Cards)- by Twin Sisters (*great family time activity*)
- The Bible For Dummies-by Geoghegan, Jeffrey (*I like this because it really helps breakdown the history of the bible*)
- Adventure Bible, NIV- by Richards, Lawrence O. (*Bought this bible for our son when he turned about 7, as a next step up bible.*)
- The Beginner's Bible: Timeless Children's Stories- by Various Authors, Kelly Pulley (*This was the bible we used for our kids when they were toddlers*)
- Prayers That Avail Much- by Germaine Copeland (*I like this book as it has various prayers for various situations or concerns.*)
- Jesus Calling: 365 Devotions For Kids- by Sarah Young (*We bought this when our kids were 7-9yrs old. After they read the devotional, we would discuss*

what they understood from the reading and then think of how they could apply to their own life.)

* * *

Other Resources

- Our kids enjoy attending Sunday school at our local church. Most times, lol. They enjoyed the fun and crafty ways that the lessons were presented. So I would consider attending church on occasion or regularly if you want, so your kids can take part in those lessons. (Note: I will say that our son, now that he is in middle school, sometimes pushes back on attending the middle school class. However, we still encourage him to visit, mainly because each time he comes out with something, he has learned that profoundly affects him. (And he actually is glad he went because he feels better about himself.) Also, we think it is vital for him to have friends through his faith. At school, he may be the only one who discusses his faith on a rare occasion. We want him to feel comfortable to have another group of friends outside of school that he can openly and regularly discuss his faith with when he gets ready. These are the main reasons we encourage him to attend.)
- The Bible App. I like that this app not only has devotional and study plans for me, but they also offer plans that are geared towards kids and families.
- Pinterest is a great resource, which I regularly use when looking for bible study at home lessons or worksheets for the kids.

About the Author

I am just a child of God, trying to live in accordance to God's Will as best I can. (Grateful that God grants me Grace while I figure it all out, lol.) I have always been a spiritual person, and I believe that having a personal relationship with God is more important than religion. However, I practice Christianity because that is where God has led me along my spiritual journey.

I love engaging in just about anything that lets me indulge my creative side. I enjoy sewing, baking, cooking, and making wreaths. I also spend a lot of time with my family just hanging out with family friends and our extended family. A weird fact about me is that I love excel, and sometimes take on projects for others, just for the fun of working through formulas. I am also a huge fan of Halloween, and all the things that come along with the holiday. (I have been known to try and sneak up my decorations mid-August, lol)

This is my first book, but I have several other spiritual books in the works. If you enjoyed and found this book helpful consider joining my mailing list to be notified once they are complete!

Thanks for taking the time to read this labor of love, and I pray that it is a blessing to you and your family.

You can connect with me on:

- https://www.kelimarie.com
- https://twitter.com/elikmarie
- https://www.facebook.com/elikmarie
- https://www.instagram.com/elikmarie

Subscribe to my newsletter:

- https://www.kelimarie.com

www.ingramcontent.com/pod-product-compliance
Lightning Source LLC
La Vergne TN
LVHW051427080426
835508LV00022B/3283